Among Ruins

Also by Winston F. Bolton

What the Air Might Say, 2013

Among Ruins

Poems by Winston F. Bolton

Cherry Grove Collections

Published by Cherry Grove Collections
P.O. Box 541106
Cincinnati, OH 45254-1106

ISBN: 9781625491435
LCCN: 2015945057

Poetry Editor: Kevin Walzer
Business Editor: Lori Jareo

Visit us on the web at www.cherry-grove.com

for Laura

Table of Contents

IV — Among the Wrack

I
About Light

About Light

Everything about light
concerns me.
Light before dawn,
before color.
The first light
that creeps onto
the mattress ticking.

Sunset, Route 106

Pure uncanny blue,
not the blue of cloudless day,
but lustrous lined,
framed with salmon pink.

To know it is no driven work
of plan or mind,
but freely given, as rain or snow.

This love laid bare,
this hint of something more.

While We Talked

While we talked, it grew dark,
the phone lit by a single lamp.

Up and down the street
house lights came on,

TVs tuned to the weather,
the news. . . .

Above a cover of broken cloud,
the cup of night fills.

October Poem

The day goes
into golden afternoon,
deep ocher afternoon
slant with shadow,
like a woman unwinding
her hair.

Elemental, silver drain
of color,
of crayon drawn and wash blue
tinctured enemy of peace;
of picture pink and blood red
ivory horn, iron,
and ultimate disuse.

Bare are her limbs,
and bare are her dreams
if dreams be good.

Oh, she goes, the day
as to a lover,
letting her hair upbraid
her innocence
down backs of trees
that follow to her rest.

Night-Leaning Woman

Leaning in the moonlight,
in the moon-lit window,

she casts shadows down,
listening to a sound

past the cut-out trees.
Hands in the folds

of the parted drapes,
eyes upon the ground.

The slender form,
shadowed back and hair,

head thrust slightly forward
beyond shoulders.

Into the shadowed night,
shadows chasing round

the bell-like tone,
one note floating there.

O Risen Moon

Some said of cheese,
some of silver . . .

those who brought bits home,
of stone and dust.

Moon of long vagaries,
O risen Moon.

Full tonight, round,
ragged with cloud,

peeking with troubled face
over rooftops

a warm summer's evening,
O cold and barren moon.

Distant, unconcerned,
a still bell

the color of old iron
loud with lost ringing.

Like a sound
a train leaves on the rail.

Night Train

Out of a blister of light,
the night train shrieking
down thrumming rails . . .
over ties and stones
on iron feet,
like hooves striking sparks,
it came,
tormented and tormenting.

Men shrank before the
glowing apparition,
and small boys gladdened.

The bell clanging
its ponderous sound,
the great drivers
hissing steam,
and the giant heart
pounding within,
sliding into the station,
a terrible writhing tamed.

Night Passes Without Sleep

O beautiful moon, O bella bella luna,
rosy in hidden light, tinted by the sun.

Through the open window, little choking sounds
up from the swamp the wild turkeys haunt.
They come, leaving all behind: the trees
in which they roost, the moon among blots
of branch, cicada song.

O dove, O small wild pigeon in your cote.
O feathered air, O concinnity, douceur,
thing of air, of easeful flight, of rest.

Where is the sleep that follows chirping dusk?

Walking the Dark

Little fist size, two-step
engine,

steady tread of the heart.
Arrives like a valentine

walking the dark.

Night Hawks Revisited

This late night restaurant
is a Hopper setting.
The emptiness of a
plate glass window,
the several customers
planted upon stools,
a cook in disenchanted white
among his gleaming pipes
and stainless surfaces.

This view shouts of silence,
the fixity of a life
from which the pith is drawn.
The street beyond, empty.
Not even a scabby cat
in the foreground.

Nothing moves. Nothing.

3:00 A.M.

Three in the morning:
the hour of the wolf.
Something I cannot feel
pushes me.

Time at my back pushing,
invisible,
as behind a veil,
like a steady rain
beating on a blind face.

A Dream of Water

The road unwinds ahead: a semi
leans into the banked curve.

The mournfulness of the wet,
the mean sad streaky windshield,

the dreary swing of wipers
mindless in their task.

They say to dream of water
means a breakthrough.

But what of the downpour
beaten back by rubber and steel?

The wash like an arras drawn aside,
drawn aside, drawn aside. . . .

Halley's Comet

Out on an icy march of space
The great head turns, doubles back
In a slow revolve along its track,
Toward a blue and shining face;
Gathering to itself the dust
Of Caesar's eyelids, and the grace
An ancient assayed to place
Once upon his marble bust.

Beaten Thin

I am gold,
beaten thin, a membrane.
Through me the sun shines,

the sun that comes
dripping out of the wet Atlantic.

I wait in the night
for daybreak, for the beating
to begin.

The Moons of Landscape

for Vincent van Gogh

What circles about what woods,
what fields, what grasses,
heaps of landmass!

The tugging and unseen
with great spaced eyes
that never close.

With skies their own
that match the matchless blue,
the slurried

moons of landscape rolling,
rolling just outside the frame,
beyond the painter's brush,

without a name.

A Cold Brocade

It's detail that we want:
the stars are pins of light,
pale patterns in the sky.

They replicate each night
for us, for us only,
a cold brocade, a far fire

against the general dark.
The Archer and the Bear
stand up against the world.

II
Beneath All Things

From Astoria

We have left the Peninsular,
Mary's classless society, dead fishers' wives,
heroes of the coast incised on the marine wall
beneath the bridge's abutment.

A bridge seeming to lead nowhere
as it spans the Columbia.
We have touched the country's westmost edge,
where beach sand soft as pumice

entombs what remains of skeletal ships —
a wreck-made landmark jutted in segments,
this sour upthrust, sea-filled hollows of pipe,
ribbed iron, enough to know what was bow.

Enough to ask of the past some remembrance:
the *Corps of Discovery,* Lewis and Clark,
the movement west . . . a people, our own driven
Indians, choused from their moment in Time.

Invitation

Return to the wigwams, campfires
Burning brightly, to the woodlands,

On the Trail of Elder Brother —
Of the Micmac, of their nation

In these pages, written by one:
Runningwolf, no patronymic,

His name given by the chieftain.
Here, turn back to the old days,

To the lodge and to the sachem,
To the Beaver and the Turtle,

Pathways through the woodland trodden.
To the shining coasts unfettered

By the great ships of the English —
Hairy, foreign, all despoilers!

Return to a past made simple,
To the padding feet unheard.

I Want To Dress Like a Cowboy

I want to dress like a cowboy,
As I did when I was young.
I want to feel on my hip again
The weight of my cap gun.
And set my hat at a cocky slant
And kill an Indian.

I want to dress like an Indian,
Who didn't dress much at all.
And creep about as silent as
A shadow on the wall.
And when I'm hit never shout
Or cry out when I fall.

On the Possibility of There
Being Evil in the World

This morning I felt like throwing a rock
at one of the old nail factory
windows.

Just one shot.
One good shot —
So many windows already broken.

I, who never
broke a window
just for the hell of it.

Just for the thrill
of hearing glass shatter,
of seeing another

shapeless piece of the dark.

Beneath All Things

The empty Chair awaits, profiled in darkness.
They are killing Sacco and Vanzetti again.
We have seen this all before,
The tragic story that does not alter with retelling.
How impeccably they dressed to die with dignity,
Their eloquent words of good-bye.

February weeps, old snow melting on the lawn.
The icicle at my window, the length of a sabre,
Has snapped.
And sparrows peck at invisible specks
Of the sustenance that lies beneath all things.

I reach for my jacket and overshoes
To join my friends for the film.
We go seeking some speck of justice,
Or its dark sister outrage at best, hearts
Dancing on anarchism's thin, raw edge.

Caver

What urges him to worm
through cracks and crevices,
as though to find the home
from which he came?

A lightless, narrow space
that never sees the sun,
with nothing but his face
before him.

The Gatherers

If rumors are true,
they no longer are rumors;
facts speak for themselves.

There, where the cascade of water
spills through the gorge —
bones whitened

so thoroughly,
as if intentionally cleansed
for our inspection.

Oh, the flesh that once
rode them, gathering heat
under the same sun!

Delicate Instrument Inside

Carefully they lower
Into the wooden, outer box
The product of their labors, stenciled
"DELICATE INSTRUMENT."
Carefully they secure
The inner cover locks.
They will never see
The risen creature.
It has gone from them this moment,
Labeled "delicate."
Oh, how delicate,
The serial, dark going
Of these instruments
To that far distant place!
Like the gold inlay with Pharaoh,
Like the little jars beside him,
Like the myrrh and frankincense.
The chamber sealed in stone,
The toil-collected tons . . .
The dark journey beyond
That no one understands.

Torn from the Sky

To go quickly,
bright as a burn.
To enter night

as to enter the Sun,
streaking light
across a *Newsweek* cover.

Bright fireballs trailing,
each white flaming arc,
flat close up, a furious motion.

Those
lifting beyond themselves
out of Earthweight,

where the starry connaissance
unrolls, and the terminator
slides silently under.

Those
who rode the last wave down
to a flattened field.

The Last Voyage of the Titanic

The last voyage of the Titanic —
also the first.

First and last . . . there's something
poetic in that.

And no one knew,
no prophet telegraphed ahead

as the iceberg, preoccupied,
patiently waited.

Other things on its mind:
the dread of melting,

becoming nothing, in the dark night
as it edged slowly southward,

one with the immense ocean,
its restlessness, its upheavals.

And the great ship so confident,
so confidently approaching.

First Kill

The deer turns in the snow as though
her broken-field running were foil
to the slug in the belly,

abruptly lurches and falls.
Eyes open, glassy with small drops
of condensation like tears

not blinked away: first kill of the season.
He is ecstatic
at this good, good stroke of luck.

Warm as life, her body a large grey
mitten wrinkling with passing life,
eyes blind to sight.

Just so, do all in time
stumble down, slug in the belly,
wrapped around a great transient pain.

Coming as going, and going for all
we know but prelude to birth, being
spilled out hot as blood again.

Trench Love

That love which bears no name,
born in the blood and muck.

The shot-off face —
machine-gun harvesting.

That love struck deeper than
for wife, mother. . . .

Ties not of blood,
nor the burning in the blood,

but the burning.

Bayonet

A woman would never
have invented
the bayonet.

It is a man's
weapon, meant to humiliate.
Twelve inches

of cold steel
in the belly — like a
metal prick.

Soldiers All

What can I do but move
From folly to defeat,
And call that sorrow sweet . . . ?

"Someone Talking to Himself"
   — Richard Wilbur

Imagining the worst above the best,
The soldier sends himself ahead to war.
The worst comes fast, in silence, like a chore
Performed by someone else. A bitter test
From which his eager body recoils lest
It carry him away from the uproar
Back to when he tottered across the floor
Where arms awaited him, and later rest.
A soldier lives and dies one of a team.
Plimpton said a soldier's job's to die, sure
As army ants surge forth, a living beam
Into the face of death, which none abjure,
Unlike the rest of us in this dark dream.
But we must love what we cannot endure.

O Nagoya!

At night in my bunk, the Quonset hut
unnaturally quiet, nearly empty.
I thought how easy to live like this
forever, awaiting assignment, without orders.

I rose early and after breakfast
would investigate the city
in my freshly laundered uniform,
shoes shined: *ke tō,* the hairy foreigner.

I met their smiles, incredulous; a people
who four years before survived
incessant bombing. And to the south,
Hiroshima. . . .

I, who carried with me to Japan
the searing mark of power,
a callow kid who could not yet —
not then — have understood.

Shrapnel

Years later, emerging
from wrist, from leg,
from somewhere deep inside
the old arthritic body.

That hard walk across Europe
to reach the Rhine . . . Paul
this morning sits across from me,
bald head pink as a June rose.

Greek Against Greek

Greek against Greek, that is the sad, bad truth,
that in the bone the battle lines are drawn:
all warring has its origin at home.

Persians — nameless others — repelled by men
too fierce in their small numbers for mere men,
learned to their sorrow they had struck at gods.

Yet fat peace, once restored, turned gods to men;
then Spartans swung upon Athenians,
and the true war, the warring self, began.

Following a Fever

for Cèsar Vallejo

They wanted a Republic —
a dome, you see,
of many-colored glass.
A cloth of flannel
under which a moth
becomes a giant fly
of many lights.

What they got was this:
40 years of ant life
under the dictator.

And the Emperor . . .

Grassy berms, hollows,
north and south.
Two billion man-hours
built Hadrian's wall.

The Old Man stayed on
till it was done.
Then back to Rome
to build the Pantheon.

His architect sworn
to suicide.
The emperor, it is said,
chased butterflies.

Sun Tzu's "Defeat"

I had taken my treasure
across the river Yi
before my enemy provoked me
to anger.

I did not act on my anger,
but yet believed that by this
provocation he had won,
before a blow was struck.

N.B. Sun Tzu *The Art Of War,* circa 500 B.C.E.

In Failing Light

To be at peace at last,
but not *to be.*
To be a vase in China
or Nepal.

Energy, neither created
nor destroyed,
persisting only
as antecedence

to all we once were. . . .
To be unspun,
scattered as the star stuff
we came from.

In failing light, to fall,
to tumble down.
A ball of yarn the kitten
has undone.

III
Ark and Alcove

Attic Stair

It takes slightly more
than a gentle pull upon the dangling cord
to swing the white-faced panel down from
the ceiling,
            revealing stair
folded upon stair.

All the dark spills down.

Laddered sections, quite secure,
rest squarely on the floor,
like the clam on shore
its single foot
            extended.

My Sister

Sometimes her presence
comes upon me,
the way she would speak;
an image, a word.
Words, perhaps, and the air
of her being close.
Not a memory, but a presence.

"Brecky," she would say
to the dog and cat, for "breakfast."
And her smile, soft, indulgent.
Yet quick to anger, to lash out,
to hurt.

She never held a grudge,
but held the world at bay,
backing further into herself
each day until
there was nowhere left
to go.

Hanging the May Basket

It was all hushed, and our breaths
a kind of singing.
The basket, waiting at the door,
with its ribbons, its glorious surprises.
And our voices rising up like flowers
among shadows.

Always at evening.
We would ring the bell,
then hide and wait for that one
to come out and find us,
while the long light died
and one by one the widows lit.

Looking Down the Path

Nothing down there but the wind,
the ragged edge of fall.

The wind and crumbling remains
of the old rec hall.

A ring of tall grass and a few pines
glistening along the path.

The far fringe of trees is all that's left,
the whole, transformed, alien.

The county land sold off,
the pond drained and filled.

We cannot go to the pond again.
In my mind's eye I see it, see

the road taken, circle round again
to the place where I often sat alone

in the late reach of afternoon,
watching the dark water

of the sluice gate, the view across
wind-shaken water, the cat's-paws,

little still pools. That scene
rising before me of a sudden,

like a frame picked from
a stuttering path of film.

Played Without Sound

This hour, my fingers flying across
these keys recording no clear tone,
like an instrument played without sound

for the player alone, who is the listener.
How far away and yet how it returns,
trivial and insular, painted on my mind;

preserved for all the time that remains,
one frame, and frame by frame
the little scene drops slowly back again.

The woman at the door, stranger
who spoke with my mother
in a serious voice about me.

I started school the same year
as my younger sister. We would
be together, our mother said.

Terrified of the teacher, the children,
I played hooky — repeating a grade.
Little fool, escaping to the station,

the draw of the tracks; I'd wait for the freights
to rumble past. The nurse would come
and take me home. Still vivid . . .

the little copse that trailed beside the window
of her car. Like a dream it stands:
lovely little flock of trees,

the cloudless reach of sky, the damp grass.
From this has come the mind that
wet its pants.

Harvest

To run barefoot again
in the cold damp grass
when summer is past
and the harvest in.

The harvest in, tinned
and on the shelves.
And the great pumpkins
rolled into piles.

I have stood alone
upon the meadow
in first light and watched
night gather up her stars,

and wondered, when did
time take me by the hand
and say, Old man,
this is where you are.

Among Ruins

I've come to find the little boy I left
Among those ruins,
Where time for him had ceased.
Here birch and pine have overgrown
A father's death, the intervening years.

Eyes fixed upon the sanatorium
I see him once again, standing alone
Before the TB hospital's stucco walls,
Whose wings flung out like sails —
So like a ship in his imagination,
The clipped green lawn a sea.

He saw his father, contagion-cautious,
At a distance. Had the man
Really smiled? Had he waved,
Or merely coughed
Before retiring to his ward?
— The grave within.

At the Plymouth County Hospital

Less now than ever,
the patients gone,
the tall rooms emptied out;
nothing but echoes.

Less now than ever,
small noises in the halls,
vacant as the memory of pain.

Less now than ever,
ice snapping in the overhangs,
roof tiles shifting.

In Mayflower Cemetery

Silence may play
as much a part in it
as any fine display
that stirs the mind
and draws the soul
out fine.

Silence may be
the whole of it.
Such silence as
we cannot know,
pressed to this world,
where every blade of grass
holds up a tinkling cymbal
as we pass.

The joy of it
may lie not in rest
but silence.
Silence such as none
had guessed
in sun, in rain, in snow.

The Essential White

After a day's snowfall
the high road to town
is one with the field.
Trees bend like burdened men,
and the pond has lost its edge.

Snow comes soundlessly,
the essential white.
And a stillness,
like the quieting of limbs
after a long night of struggle,
eyes staring at nothing more
than an emptied sky.

L'Infinito

A free translation of
Giacomo Leopardi's poem.

Always dear to me, this knobbly hill,
this low hedge which almost blocks
the horizon. Yet in my dreaming eye
boundless spaces reel away in quietude;
the silences deepen like the lowest notes
of a barely beating heart. And the wind
rushes through the underbrush with wings
its own, its speech an infinite motion.
And when the high coarse wind assaults
the trees, I hold that tumult up against
infinite silence. And eternity comes near,
all that has gone before, all that is to come
cross paths, beats upon my heart. O sea,
how sweet to give my whole self to thee.

Meadow

Someone
has taken my meadow,
seized the hair of the moment:
a cement foundation,
the outline of a house. . . .

Here, in fall, horse chestnuts
slicked the ground beneath our feet.
And the mystery of old cars
in tall grass, rusting.
My woods, my meadow!

Soon the space will narrow,
the door will close.
Do the throats of birds choke
when spring comes empty-
handed? Who measures
the indignity of sparrows?

For Ernest Wight

The perfect view will not last.
      — Richard Eberhart

It matters little, you said, the view from
the terrace, the patio —
unless its compass opens to the heart.

That said, years passed.
Older now, I continuously harrow my head —
While you, I hear, have also drifted south.

Remember the sea's riff — at times deep,
at others the ding of a spoon? Sometimes
it all comes back, each wave tipped with sun.

The swallows this summer failed to come;
the luffing roof's gone. You were right,
living rooms must be within the soul's grasp.

Such Was My Dream

for Faye

I am too happy in my happiness.
For you, dear one, are happiness to me.
Soft blooms perfume the air, and angels press
An eiderdown. I've seen the burly sea

Smile like a child because you watched nearby,
As though some ancient god poured forth his coin,
Indifferent to time's thief, patient and sly,
Waiting to alter, waiting to purloin.

Such was my dream — was it a dream? The sun
Upon us bright and full that afternoon,
You close beside me. Never was there one
More happy, with you my constant boon.

But then my heart grew weak, my footsteps slow,
Knowing that you must leave, or I first go.

Friend of the Future

My eyes have forgotten.
Like the half dead, I hug
my last secrets.
— Theodore Roethke

"Dick Ewell?" I heard,
in the local food market, turning
to see familiarity fade
in the stranger's pleasant face.

"Sorry," I said, thinking
it must be the beard. Often, it seems,
I'm mistaken for another.

The tall, slim man smiled and pushed on.
I watched him at the checkout counter,
unloading his cart, thoughtfully
placing provisions where the clerk
might more easily scan them.

In a way he did look familiar. Someone
perhaps I'd like to know, to sit with
as a friend on a lonely morning
in the town's coffee shop.

A comfortable friend, a friend
you might speak with about
anything at all. As our paths widened,
an emptiness grew.

Firehouse

Weymouth Landing

Closed now. Saying,
Go away. Call 911.
Call anyone but me.
I will never ring again,
echoing with firehouse clamor,
wooden door thrown open
                    like a mouth.

Those lovely old stones,
quarried from Quincy,
rough-hewn, tawny:
golden browns and tans.
Like sunlight and shadow.

The Barn

The strap hangs
from the broken sled.
The horse
stolen long ago
dreams no more.
The barn
once taller than rain
sits down in the storm.

Visitations

1.

I stood there, in Emily's big square bedroom,
looking out the window at fields she followed,
where those paths had taken her. . . .
Vintage figure, the long white dress, the parted hair.
From her wooden desk, I walked down through
the unattended garden, wild as wool,
taking the path that bore her to her final rest,
touching one wrought iron ink-black post,
thinking of all the words she'd sent ahead.

2.

And in a book of photographs I stroked the bite-size
gougings in the beams above Neruda's cellar bar,
where friends had left their names, initials, runes.
That ship-like house perched on the sea's moist lip,
quiet now, between the tourist flows, the ebb
and tide of curiosity. Each bottle, shell, and curio,
each wooden maiden, ship's wheel, painted horse
his eye had held, left in its place, accustomed and alone.
The two small doors that closed on poet and dame,
the speech of spray and wind.

Ark and Alcove

They speak to me, old things, of their time:
old books, old lamps, old chairs. . . .
From the dump today a wooden hanger,
the kind my father had in his chiffonier;
shirts and pants suspended in neat rows.
I wish I had it still, for its spaciousness,
its smell.

The record cabinet beneath our Victrola,
shellac blended with wood and polish.
I'd tug and swing the small door open
on the sly, breathe deeply the odor.
The scent of timelessness: of ark and alcove.

IV
Among the Wrack

Blue Estuary

for Louise Bogan

Where currents cross
like hair drawn wet,
the large sea
contracts in her eye.

Wind tosses off whitecaps.
Like painted dreams, steamers
poise serenely on the line.

She comes with her
unwise, heady dream
to the large sea, sees it blue,
conflicted in the offing.

Duet

1. Piano Lesson

Side by side
at your piano
we make our soft
morning racket.

What is *mezzo forte?*
Does a slur work
where fingers itch
on a hammer of change?

2. A Reed Singing

Each time we sit
at your piano
we almost touch.

Only our voices touch,
bodiless,
an urgent rise of tones

that are ours
and not ours.

3. Alone Yet Not Alone

When I am not with you
I am alone.
And when I am
with you, I am alone

Old Loves

Old loves, they line my heart
Like books once read.
Some few, I came to know.
Others sit like angels on the head
Of one small pin.
And in the dark they glow.

A Terrible Courage

Bitter as gall
the bright dream failed.

They sweat an impossible
marriage.

Once the gate gave,
the worm was within.

She ate of the power,
passed it to him.

He trailed a finger in blood,
as ancient as myth.

Blind as old drays
the two of them haul

a terrible courage.

The House of Ostrogodo

after *An Untenable Situation*
    — Pablo Neruda

In the house of Ostrogodo, weariness
with the comings and goings of corpses.
The family moved out into the garden.
They ate the pomegranate of displeasure,
the plum of emptiness, the banana of durance.
They ate the fruit of wax, and something furry,
like a mouse.

That family of gnashers, habitual mourners.
Howling, at last they tore the drapes
from ancestral walls, fashioned cerements
of window shades. The living died on
a berry of bitter taste, and the dead —
— alive to death.

The Wind and the Lizard

Dry as a river bed
only the wind visits,
only the wind and the lizard,
where words once flowed

in such profusion
my pen moved
scarcely fast enough
to catch all that was said.

Now nothing comes
but dry ruinous thoughts:
the wind, and the lizard
gasping in sun.

The Face of Sleep

Sleep is such a naked act,
the face goes limp,
the jaw falls slack.

The self looks inward,
if at all, and we
are rendered invisible.

A Body in Repose

I reach behind me,
feel the crack in my arse,
that place beneath poetry.
Think of the split in self which drives
all toward the ancient difference.
One, yet out of one, many.

Feel around the moist exit,
the primal earthiness, embrace
of things moon down, of stars
long lost, where cilia first had swum.

I reach behind me — O stew of life!
O rump even of man and every nation.
Lap, lap, the old sea, father
and gods, which once we bowed to
where they rose.

Little Augean stable each bears
to the end, where fancy sinks, this
flower, this stinking stump.

Narcissus

Those who gaze
at themselves in mirrors
do not love *that* self,
but seek an identity
beyond their own.

They are as desperate
for that essence
as you or I would be
with an absence
of reflection.

So Many Turns of the Head

We wear them out, our parts.
So many turns of the head,
So many flexings of the wrist —
Ups and downs of stairs.
The hopping toad within the breast
Must rest at last.

Our minds, too, with their thoughts
That circle round and round
Like children's hoops before
They drop. Butterflies,

After so many flutterings,
Fold their pretty wings
And do not rise.

On Running Empty

We do not feel time passing.
It flows. It flows
away before us.

I have learned with
increasingly keen
awareness to chew
and chew that rind
which holds all
that is left.

It flows, it flows
away before me.
Friends,
very strangers,
going, going,
heedlessly from view.

Yesterday

I tossed yesterday
to my beast.

It gnawed all day,
it gnawed all day

down to a little
night end.

I Weep

But why are you grieving?
Did you know Monsieur Proust?
    — Comte Henri Greffulhe

I weep for the lowliest who weep,

no matter the woman, the man, the child.
I weep for the butler of Comte Henri,
found weeping after the day Proust died.

I weep for the alley, for the street
with sad lights dimmed; I weep for all
who do not weep for me. I am
the weeper for whom one may pull

the tolling bell.

Flowers

Hand to the living the bright faces,
Hand to them your green cut sheathes
In all their colors now.
It's the living that want flowers,
Not the dead in their dust and moil.

What Not Is

Pessoa says Death
is not slumber.
No, it is not sleep.

Death is absence of an absence,
the absence of feeling
in a feeling creature.

Like the pool of light
to which cows come,
mistaking light for water.

Out There

The sea pervades itself —
but only out there.
Coming upon land, it overgrows,

simpers, lumbers, spills —
crashes, tears, fills up
the good reflective pools

where mussels, periwinkles, gulls
gather; here osprey build.
Out there, it is itself. Mad by turns,

mountainous at wind's command,
conveying the sense
of an all pervading absence.

In Among the Wrack

The shore today is bare, hard-driven.
And the pebbles, crushed, crumbled
— hear them grab in among the wrack.
Now in this place, too, the same voice:
Here before, here before . . . here after.

Water to Water

To quiet oneself
in rolled cold shocking green.

To pass
as through a window —
out of light, unbeing.

Water to water, folding
the wings down.

Lest We Forget

But we do, forget.
As the wave, which collects

itself for the shore,
becomes no more

than a trifling eddy, spent.
Or the anguish of loss,

tamed by rain-etched stones
to a studied indifference.

Acknowledgments

I wish to acknowledge the help and support I have received in the preparation of *Among Ruins* from my friend and editor Faye George, whose enthusiasm for this collection, informed criticism, and devoted efforts have guided it to completion.

And I am enormously grateful to Janet Locke, for her time, patience, and expertise in formatting the manuscript for production.

About the Author

WINSTON F. BOLTON

WINSTON F. BOLTON was educated at
Northeastern and at Boston University, where he
studied with Robert Lowell. He is the author of
What the Air Might Say (Rock Village Publishing,
2013). His poems have appeared in a variety of
anthologies, journals and periodicals, including
Poetry. His work is represented in college-level
textbooks, *An Introduction to Literature,* 12th
edition (2001), and *Literature for Composition,* 6th
edition (2003), published by Addison Wesley
Longman. A retired technical writer and editor, he
lives in Halifax, Massachusetts.

CPSIA information can be obtained at www.ICGtesting.com
Printed in the USA
BVOW11s0755270715

410216BV00001B/7/P